PUPPY LOVE
by
Kate Tym

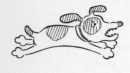

If you are an animal lover then look out for these books all published by Element Children's Books:

Talking to Animals

Animals Make You Feel Better

Star Signs – An Astrological Guide for You And Your Pet

A Yoga Parade of Animals

PUPPY LOVE
True Life Stories of Animal Friends

Kate Tym
Illustrated by John Blackman

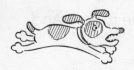

ELEMENT
CHILDREN'S BOOKS

SHAFTESBURY, DORSET · BOSTON, MASSACHUSETTS · MELBOURNE, VICTORIA

*For Muffy, Errol, Tilly, Tabbetha, Ken, and Eric,
and all the other animals I have loved.*

First published in Great Britain in 1999 by
Element Children's Books
Shaftesbury, Dorset SP7 8BP

Published in the USA in 1999 by
Element Books, Inc.
160 North Washington Street,
Boston MA 02114

Published in Australia in 1999 by
Element Books and distributed by
Penguin Australia Limited,
487 Maroondah Highway, Ringwood,
Victoria 3134

Cover photograph: Telegraph Colour Library
Cover design by Mandy Sherliker

Text design by Dorchester Typesetting Group Ltd
Printed and bound in Great Britain by
Biddles Ltd, Guildford and King's Lynn

British Library Cataloguing in Publication data available.
Library of Congress Cataloging in Publication data available.

ISBN 1 901881 34 2

Introduction

How could anybody not love animals? They're furry, they're fluffy, they're feathery, they're fun – and they're absolutely chock-full of love! In collecting these stories I've discovered just what a wonderful world it is out there, where animals look out for their human friends and people respond by trying to give their animals the best life they possibly can. Even as I type this, my cat Muffy is engaged in a battle of wits with a rubber band and as I watch her, I know why people love their animals . . . it's because they're just so darned loveable!

Kate Tym, July 1998

Splodge the Cat with a Good Education

WHEN Mark Trimmer was a little boy his mother got him two kittens – Splodge and Smudge. Splodge was splodgy and Smudge was smudgy. Splodge was white with thick splodges of brown and black dotted over her sleek coat. Smudge was a lovely smoky gray color. They were cousins.

From the beginning Smudge and Splodge showed great differences in personality. Smudge was a lazy thing, happy to lie on top of the fish tank where the light beneath

made the lid all warm. Splodge, on the other hand, would prefer to sit in front of the fish tank, eyes alert, her tail flicking restlessly as she watched the bright tropical fish flitting back and forth.

Smudge couldn't catch a bird to save her life but Splodge was a grade A mouser. Mark's mother was always yelling out over some or other dead creature that Splodge had happily trailed into the house as a present for her beloved Mark.

When the kittens had first arrived, Mark went to the playgroup around the corner from his house and sometimes, at playtime outside in the yard, he would look over at the fence and see Splodge sitting up on top of it. Mark would walk over and Splodge would jump down and rub up against her good friend's legs. The other children would soon come over and Splodge would be the center of attention, lapping up the strokes and the adoring words.

When Mark was six he moved from the playgroup to the little school further down the road. On his first day, he walked proudly along with his mother. "You look like a proper big boy, now," she said, patting the top of her son's head. They reached the school gates and Mark was just about to let go of his mother's hand and step through them, when he spotted a sleek shape trotting behind her. "Splodge!" he yelled, "what are you doing here?"

"Oh, silly Splodge," his mother said gently, "she's followed you to school. Come on Splodge," she said, stooping and picking up the protesting cat. "Back home we go."

Mark trotted happily into school; trust Splodge to follow him to make sure he was OK. The whole family laughed about it when they got home. "Splodge'll get used to it," his mother said, laughing. "What a funny cat."

But Splodge didn't get used to it. She followed Mark on his second day at his new school, on his third day, and every day after that. At first Mark's mother would pick Splodge up and carry her back home, but all that happened was that at lunch time Mark would come out into the playground and find his furry friend already out there waiting for him. As Mark got older, his mother stopped walking with him to school and as Mark and his friends dawdled along,

swinging their bags, a familiar figure would be shadowing them every step of the way.

When Mark was eight, he moved into Miss Ellis's class – she was a real cat lover. It wasn't long before Splodge was welcomed into the classroom and even had her own special basket, with a warm fluffy blanket to curl up on during lessons. Mark and all his friends wished they could be just like Splodge and sleep right through boring old math, instead of having to do any adding and subtracting.

The years went by at Mark's little sc[hool] and Splodge became part of the scenery[.] Mark moved up through the classes, Splodge moved with him. She trotted to school with him in the mornings, joined him outside at recess and then, at the end of the day, trotted back home with him. She'd become quite a celebrity; all the mothers looked out for her, and all the little children made a big fuss of her, wherever she went. Mark was very proud to have such a special cat.

Then came the inevitable. Mark was going to have to change schools. He was going to leave Crowhurst and move up to the bigger secondary school, on the other side of town. The whole family spent the summer holidays worrying about what to do about the "Splodge situation". "Surely she won't follow you right the way across town," Mark's mother said, although she didn't sound too sure.

September came and the leaves on the trees began to turn to the rich fall colors of gold and orange. Mark's mother made him wait outside the front door so that she could take a photo of him in his new school clothes. He tugged at the collar of his shirt

which rubbed uncomfortably against his neck, and then, he set off. The plan was in place: his mother had taken the morning off to stand guard over Splodge and as Mark headed away from the house, he couldn't help feeling a little sad and alone without his faithful shadow padding quietly at his heel. Every now and again he would turn suddenly, expecting to see Splodge happily walking behind him as usual. His heart felt heavy when he realized she wasn't there and wouldn't ever be there again. "Come on," he told himself, "you're going to high school now. What will the other kids think if you bring your cat with you every day?"

Splodge was kept in for a whole week. She howled the house down and refused to speak to Mark when he came home at the end of the day. "She's sulking," his mother said. "Don't worry, she'll get over it." But Mark wasn't so sure.

At the beginning of the second week Mark set off as usual. He walked down his road, picked up his friend Mick on the way, and headed down the hill towards the town. They were about halfway through their journey when they heard a familiar "mrrrp" behind them. They both wheeled round in excitement; "Splodge!" they cried as the cat wound herself lovingly around their legs.

"She's out of her sulk, then," Mick laughed.

"Yeah, looks like it," Mark smiled. "What am I going to do with you, eh?" he said to Splodge. "It's not like little school you know. They won't let you in here." But . . . they did!

It took some time and a number of meetings with Mark, his parents, the principal and even the School Board but, eventually, Splodge was allowed to come to school with Mark and attend lessons with him. After all, they reasoned, it wasn't as if they could stop her.

Splodge was fast becoming a celebrity in the town. Every day she would trot proudly down

the main street behind Mark. "Morning, Splodge," shopkeepers would say.

"Hello there, Mark, how's my lovely Splodge?" old ladies would inquire, fishing a tasty morsel out of their handbags for the little cat.

The local paper even did a story about Splodge and took photos around the school. The principal tried to make it sound as if it was all his idea, something about teaching the children caring and responsibility. But everyone knew the truth: Splodge went to school because she wanted to and not because any principal thought it was a good idea.

When Mark was 18, he left school and went off to university in another town. He missed Splodge, but he knew she was happy and well looked after at home. It was fifteen years since he'd got her as a little kitten and she'd followed Mark to school from the day he started to the day he finally left and then, it seemed, she knew her work was done and she was happy to curl up with old stay-at-home Smudge on top of the warm fish tank. Her roaming days were over, but everyone still thought of her as the cat that went to school.

Did you know...?

 Cats have really good hearing, and can often pick up sounds we don't even hear. Like, is that the sound of a can of my favorite kitty dinner being opened?!

Gunter, a Very Posh Pooch

An Austrian Countess loved her German Shepherd dog, Gunter, so much that she wanted to make sure that he was well cared for after she had died. She left Gunter $100,000 in her will to ensure that he could have all his doggy desires fulfilled for the rest of his days.

Does Your Puppy Love You?

You love Fido, but does he feel the same way about you? Find out with the following quiz if it's you your pup or pussy cat loves . . . or just your food!

....

1. You're on the phone to your best buddy and the chat's taking longer than expected. Does your pet

a. stay in the kitchen yowling at your dad for some din-dins?

b. come over to you and give you a tap with its paw?

c. sit down and stare at you with its ears pointing forward?

....

2. You're tidying your bedroom and have to shift your pet from the middle of your crumpled duvet. Does it

a. race out of the room like a rocket?

b. roll onto its back, stretch out its legs, and lie there watching you?

c. stand up, flatten its ears and drop its tail down?

3. Your pet's sitting down next to the TV. You go over and give it a stroke. Are its ears usually

a. twitching around nervously?
b. flat down against its head?
c. pointing forwards and slightly outwards?

4. You're having a sing-along to your favorite CD. Does your pet

a. stick up its ears, look at you, then leave the room?
b. sit up, tip its head back and join in the song?
c. tilt its head to one side and look at you, puzzled?

5. You come in late from an after-school activity. As soon as you get through the door, is your pet

a. jumping up at you in excitement?
b. lying in the hall, head on paws, with droopy eyelids and floppy ears?
c. nowhere to be seen?

6. Your pet's out catching some rays in the garden. You go to join it. When it stands up to greet you, is its tail

a. curving gently down then up again at the tip?

b. lowered and fluffed up a bit, like a feather duster?

c. outstretched, but twitching a bit at the end?

7. You've just got in from school. Your pet's asleep in the living room. Is it

a. flat out on its back with its tummy bared to the world?

b. curled up in a tight ball under a chair?

c. lying on its front, tail limp and head on its paws?

8. You've flopped into your favorite armchair and have just started really getting into *Puppy Love*; will your pet

a. leap on your lap and sit gazing at you over the top of your book?

b. go for a snooze with its back against the chair?

c. jump on the sofa for a more private nap?

9. You're brushing your hair in front of your mirror, while your pet has a laze on your bed. When you turn around to look at it, is it

a. staring back at you with great big pupils?

b. gazing lazily at you with its eyes only half open?

c. Looking around the room at the interesting things on your walls?

10. You're glued to the goggle box, when your pet comes in to share the view. Does it

a. come over, lie on its back and start wriggling playfully?

b. come up and shove its furry mush right in your face?

c. swipe you with a paw and run straight back out of the room?

Paw-pal scores

1. A 0	B 10	C 5		2. A 0	B 10	C 5		
3. A 5	B 0	C 10		4. A 0	B 10	C 5		
5. A 10	B 5	C 0		6. A 10	B 0	C 5		
7. A 10	B 0	C 5		8. A 10	B 5	C 0		
9. A 0	B 10	C 5		10. A 5	B 10	C 0		

25 or less

Scaredy cat

Your pet knows who wears the pants in your house . . . you do! It's good to be the boss, but remember, it's good to take it easy too. You don't want to turn your dog or mog into a quivering wreck! Shy and sensitive creature that it is, your pet still needs to learn

how to relax in your company. Try to spend more quiet time around it and remember, don't stare at it too much as this can be seen as a threat rather than the look of undying adoration we know it's meant to be!

25–60

Part-time poochy pal

You've got that fickle sort of critter who just can't make up its mind. One minute it's up for love and hugs and the next it finds all your affection a bit of a bore. If there are strangers around it'll

turn to you for comfort and protection, but the rest of the time it's more than happy hanging out on its own and letting you get on with your wacky old human life.

60 and over
True love

Your pet's as happy as Larry and likes nothing better than to spend its time with its favorite person in the world – and that means you! You mean everything to your critter – playmate, protector, and big best buddy. Ooooh, isn't it just great to be adored . . .? and the nice thing is, your pet only loves you because you've given it so much love too! Ahhh!

Did you know . . .?

That when your cat is a kitten you can train it to walk on a lead and harness to give it a bit of safe outdoor exercise until it's big enough to go it alone. What a lucky kitty to have such a caring friend.

We had a fresh-water mussel in our fish-tank; it didn't move for what seemed like weeks. I was so upset because I thought it had died. Then my dad's friend told us that if it died its shell would open up. I was really relieved, but I still wasn't sure if he was right, because it still didn't seem to go anywhere. Then one morning I got up and went to look in the tank and the mussel had moved right over to the other side! Now I watch out every day to see if I can spot it on the move!

Kirsty, Halifax, Nova Scotia

Did you know . . .?

 That you can keep your dog's breath fresh with special doggy toothpaste and a special doggy toothbrush. That way, you'll be able to keep Rover away from the special doggy dentist and still be able to get close enough for a quick kiss!

Amy – a Cat in the Lap . . . of Luxury

A cat called Amy lives in the lap of luxury in a top-class pet hotel in Newcastle-upon-Tyne in England. Her rich owner made arrangements before her death to ensure that Amy would live out her life in kitty comfort. Amy has her own suite, complete with en-suite bathroom (including a bath and a shower), a television, a video, and a garden area. But, of course, the most important thing Amy has is the love she gets from the people who run the hotel. They take their role very seriously and are happy to ensure that your pet gets all the love it needs even when you're not around to give it anymore.

Show your cat you love it by

Making it a special kitty toy.

Giving its fur a gentle brush.

Keeping its bowl nice and clean and always feeding it right on time.

The Story of Greyfriar's Bobby

If ever you go to Edinburgh in Scotland, there's one place you should be sure to visit, if you want to know about a little dog that won the heart of a whole city. The little dog's name is Greyfriar's Bobby and his story is one of a love that lasted a lifetime . . . and beyond.

In Edinburgh in the middle of the nineteenth century lived a man called Old Jock. It was his job to mind the cattle that were brought into the town every night, ready for the market the next day. He had a little dog – a Skye terrier – who kept him company and whom he loved very much. He called his dog Bobby.

Bobby was a friendly fellow and loved to curl up close to Jock as they sat through many a cold winter's night. And Jock would be grateful to have Bobby's warm little body pressing against his. Every morning, the long night behind them, they would go off for a warming breakfast in a local café and Bobby would enjoy tucking in to any of the scraps Old Jock left over. They spent every minute of every day and night together, inseparable friends. Neither could ever imagine life without the other. Old Jock loved Bobby and Bobby loved Old Jock.

Then in 1858 something happened to change Bobby's life for ever. The long nights sitting huddled in the cold finally took their toll on Old Jock and he died. Bobby was devastated; he and Jock had been through thick and thin together – he couldn't remember a night without the old man to snuggle up to. He followed Jock's funeral procession in misery and sat, shivering, under a toppled headstone close to the old man's grave.

At first the man who looked after the graveyard tried to shoo Bobby away, but then it became clear that the little dog meant to stay by Old Jock's side for the rest of his days. News of the little dog soon spread around the town and people were so touched by the story that they would bring Bobby bits of food to eat and he was given his own water bowl and a beautiful engraved collar and best of all, special permission to stay in the graveyard for as long as he wanted to.

Bobby remained there for fourteen long years until, in 1872, he too passed away quietly one night.

The whole of Edinburgh was in mourning. They buried little Bobby in Greyfriar's Churchyard close to the grave of Old Jock, and just outside, they built a little statue, dedicated to their favorite dog. So, if you ever go to Edinburgh and are anywhere near Greyfriar's Churchyard go and read the plaque that says:

A tribute to the affectionate fidelity of Greyfriar's Bobby. In 1858 this faithful dog followed the remains of his master to Greyfriar's Churchyard and lingered near the spot until his death in 1872.

Ahh – we love Greyfriar's Bobby!

Once when I was a baby my mom found me eating out of our dog Buster's bowl. Mom was really upset, but Buster didn't seem to mind at all!

Aaron, Texas

Did you know...?

Gerbils are very sociable creatures and don't like to live alone. So if you're going to get a gerbil . . . think again . . . and get two for double the love!

Boris – a Swine that's Doin' Fine!

Boris, the pot-bellied pig, lives in a sty with style in south eastern Wisconsin. His piggy palace has its own legal address, where he receives mail – including bills from Wisconsin Electric! His home has a central vacuuming system, and pig-height windows, and no solid barriers so that Boris is free to roam at will. And being a caring piggy, his home even has wheel-chair access for his disabled friends.

Did you know . . .?

That some short-haired doggies feel the cold and need to wrap up in a nice warm coat when they go out for walkies in winter. Very chic I'm sure!

Show your dog you love it by

Taking it for lots of nice walkies!

Taking the time to praise it for good behavior.

Giving its bedding a nice clean from time to time.

When I was about eight, our family went on holiday for two weeks and left the neighbour in charge of our two cats and two rabbits. When we came back home the neighbour said that she had come every day and that Charlie had always come for his food but Mooch was never anywhere to be seen. She was very upset and worried about him, and so were we! We opened the garage door to put the car away and there, looking very thin and dirty, was Mooch! One of his favourite places to hide was on top of the flat garage door when it was open: when we'd closed the door after we'd got the car out Mooch must have jumped down *inside* the garage. It was amazing Mooch had

survived; the vet said he must have lived off
water from condensation in the garage and
that his kidneys might be a bit damaged.
Mooch lived on to be fifteen years old (ten
years later), but I really think that was the

Did you know...?

That cats often don't
like their traveling
baskets, because they
know that whenever
they go in them,
something bad is going to happen (like
a trip to the vet's – Yikes!). So to keep
kitty happy in its traveling basket, you
can put her in there from time to time,
when nothing
unpleasant is going
to happen, and
even sit her in there
and give her a
treat. Then she'll
think her traveling
basket is a place
where nice things
happen too! And
that'll be all thanks to you know who!

first of his nine lives used up. After that, we always looked out for Mooch before closing the garage door, but he was never there again — he'd definitely learned his lesson.

Kairen, Maidenhead

Abdul the Hero

An Australian stretcher-bearer in World War I, James Simpson Kirkpatrick, used a Greek burro (donkey), called Abdul to carry the wounded soldiers after their landing in Gallipoli in Turkey, in 1915, went terribly wrong.

Kirkpatrick who became known as the "Good Samaritan of Gallipoli" placed one soldier after another on Abdul's strong back to be carried down a dangerous gully, with shots ringing out all around them. Even after

Kirkpatrick was killed Abdul kept going and was regarded as as much of a hero in the war as the soldiers who fought in it.

At the Shrine of Remembrance in Melbourne, Australia, there is a statue called 'The Man with the Donkey'. It shows Kirkpatrick supporting a wounded soldier on Abdul's back. And Abdul means so much to the Australians and New Zealanders that in 1964 he even appeared on three postage stamps which commemorated the fiftieth anniversary of the Gallipoli landing. What a wonderfully brave donkey!

I love my iguana, Eric because he scares my Auntie Sheila half to death and gives the rest of us a really good laugh!

Darren, Inverness.

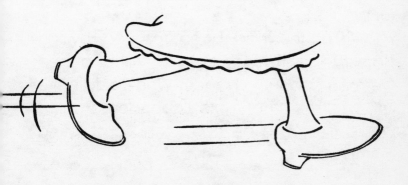

Rin Tin Tin – The Movie Star Dog

In the 1920s and 30s in America, there was one film star who was bigger than all the rest. He was so popular, that his box-office earnings alone were enough to keep Warner Brothers at the top of the movie making ladder. This most famous of movie stars was a German shepherd called Rin Tin Tin!

The public just loved him, and he got over 10,000 fan letters a week. He made over forty movies in around nine years and earned over a million dollars. He was a great daredevil and thought nothing of scaling walls and jumping through fake glass windows. But, what made him most popular was his acting ability. He could change his expression from sad, to hopeful to joyous in one frame and his public just adored him for it.

In 1918, he had been rescued by an American airman from an abandoned German dugout in France. Who could have known that that little abandoned dog would go on to be one of the best loved animals the silver screen has ever seen.

Pet Rescue

Los Angeles, in America, has long been considered the home of all new crazes. And the latest trend to take the town by storm is learning how  to give mouth to . . . snout resuscitation. People are signing up left-right-and-center to get their chops around their doggy's nose. For anyone who's worried about Rover choking on his rubber ball or getting half-drowned in the local pond, it's an absolute must. But, be warned; don't try giving your pet the kiss of life without proper training – it could be fatal!

When my dog Tigger was a little puppy he would chase his tail for hours on end. He didn't seem to realize it belonged to him. He'd spin around and around, and sometimes he'd get so dizzy he'd just fall over!

Elouise, Harrisburg

The Emperor of Japan's Cat

In around 999AD the Emperor Ichijo of Japan had a very dear cat called Myobu No Omoto. He loved his cat with all his heart. One day Myobu had to be rescued from a dog who was chasing her. The emperor was furious and he had the dog exiled from Japan and the dog's female attendant imprisoned. Now some people might think that's taking things just a little bit too far!

I love my cat, Billy, because whenever I feel sad, I can talk to Billy and he always makes me feel better.

Genevieve, Bolton

The Tamworth Two

In January 1998 Great Britain went bonkers over two little pigs who became known as the Tamworth Two. The two porky pals were brought to the nation's attention when they were taken to an abattoir where they were supposed to breathe their last. The two pigs, who later were called Butch and

Sundance after two other famous evaders of the law, were ginger Tamworth pigs, a specialty breed that, according to people who like that sort of thing, were supposed to turn into the most delicious of sausages. But . . . the Tamworth Two had other ideas. They took one look at the slaughterhouse and headed for the door.

Tamworth pigs are renowned for their intelligence and cunning and these two were no exception. They not only made it out of the door at lightning speed, but they also managed to get across a river and into some woods before the butchers had a chance to blink. The news was reported locally, and then picked up by the bigger national newspapers and television news. Soon the whole nation knew the story, and even people who loved sausages were rooting for the piggy pair never to be brought to book.

Days went by and the search was still on; locals of the town of Malmesbury, where the pigs were at large, had spotted them snuffling in their gardens, but no one had actually managed to pin the pair down. The newspapers were in a frenzy, fighting over who would eventually take the praise for saving the pigs; the army was called in and helicopters circled the woods but still the fugitives remained hidden.

In the end, it took a specially trained springer spaniel to coax the boys out of their lair, in some very thick bushes. And, one tranquillizer dart later, they were on the way to the safe haven of a petting farm. They had been bought for a substantial fee by the *Daily Mail* who had fought off offers from rival newspapers. First they were pampered

at an animal sanctuary in Wiltshire, before being moved on to a safe farm in North Wales where they are destined to live out their lives as pampered porkers at the hands of their loving and affectionate new owners.

Phew! – The whole of Britain breathed a sigh of relief; it was a happy ending for the Tamworth Two, the best-loved pigs in the whole country!

Did you know....?

Rabbits just love to be cuddled, but only if you pick them up properly. Always pick bunny up with both hands and use one hand to support its big bouncy bottom. Then Thumper will be happy to have a huggle for as long as you like.

No Greater Love Has Any Man . . .

IN November 1993 blazing fires swept across the west coast of America's exclusive Malibu area. Usually a haven of tranquility where Hollywood stars rubbed shoulders with models and millionaires, a long dry spell had triggered a number of small wildfires, which, after a time, began blazing out of control.

The British film director, Duncan Gibbins, lived there in an exclusive rented ranch. Little did he know that the beautiful place he had chosen to be his home would also be the site of his tragic and untimely death. Because when the fires that were sweeping towards him finally engulfed his home, Duncan Gibbins refused go to safety until he had first rescued Elsa, his cat.

It was only a few days earlier that Gibbins had adopted Elsa. The three-year-old Siamese blue-point was a stray in need of a home and Duncan Gibbins decided to give her a new life in the lap of luxury. But soon, the nightmare began. The out-of-control fire reached Gibbins's home. He managed to escape unscathed, but then, instantly realized that Elsa was still inside. He couldn't leave her to die, and so he went back in to save her.

He emerged in a terrible state with a badly burned Elsa. He threw himself in his swimming pool to try to soothe the terrible burns he now had on his body. But the damage had been done, and Duncan Gibbins died of his injuries soon afterwards.

A nation's hearts went out to Elsa as she lay fighting for her life in an animal shelter. She had burns on 50 percent of her body, her ears and tail were badly scorched, she was dehydrated and depressed. Calls flooded in from people all over the world that wanted to give Elsa a home. They were so moved by the terrible events that they wanted at least one good thing to come out of it, the very thing that Duncan Gibbins had died for: to keep Elsa alive.

Eventually, Elsa found a new home with a close friend of Duncan's. She felt that by looking after Elsa, she would be helping to keep Duncan's memory alive. Elsa may never really realize how much Duncan loved her. Enough to give up his own life to make sure she stayed alive.

REMEMBER – never ever go back into a burning building, or even waste time getting out in order to save your pet. Your pet wouldn't want you to lose your life on its behalf.

Did you know . . .?

Rabbits respond to a bit of a chat. If you talk gently to your rabbit it will make it feel safe

and welcome. If it responds, give it a huggle as a lovely reward. Ahhh, there's nothing more snuggly than a lovely furry bunny!

Toad Road

Along several of Britain's motorways (superhighways), tunnels have been built beneath the road surface to provide safe crossing for all creatures small and smaller but . . . most especially for toads! Toad-lovers galore have fought for safe crossings for their favorite amphibians, sick of seeing them squidged under the wheels of un-caring cars. They decided to do something about it and make sure that when Toady wants to the cross the roady, he can do it in safety!

Hounds for Hire

At an exclusive hotel in London's Mayfair, no dog-lover need ever feel lonely. If you're pining for your Poodle or lost without your Labrador the hotel can sort you out with a temporary paw-pal to keep you company during your stay. With Green Park nearby, those far away from home and missing taking their dogs for walkies can borrow the general manager's two dogs and go for a delightful stroll in a bit of central London greenery. Apparently it's a much sought after service. People really miss their pooches when they're away from home, and the company of two friendly woofers can really lift their spirits. There's nothing like a wagging tail and a wet nose to make you feel really wanted!

Did you know . . .?

If you take your dog for a walk at the same time every day, it'll get right into the habit and come and find you when it's time to go out for walkies. Ahhh – schweet!

Errol the Rat on a Diet

JANE Burnard's favorite animal in the whole world was her hooded-rat, Errol. Errol was a mainly white rat with a brown hood and saddle down his back. His nose was pink and twitchy, his eyes dark and alert, and his tail long and strong. Jane and Errol would spend as much time together as they could. Rats are very clever animals and Errol would come at the call of his name. He would climb up Jane's leg, gripping with his tail for extra support.

Jane had got Errol from one of her neighbors when he was still quite small. She'd always handled him a lot from the beginning and so he had become used to having lots of cuddles and looked forward every day to when Jane would come in from school and rush up the stairs to see him. Jane loved Errol so much, she refused to keep him in a cage. He had free run of her bedroom, his food bowl was kept topped up with all the good things he liked to eat, and he had a special toilet tray that Jane cleaned out every day – he was a very happy ratty!

Errol's day started by climbing up Jane's leg and sitting in the pocket of her dressing

45

gown. Then, they'd go downstairs together for a bowl of porridge. Jane would have hers in a big bowl and Errol would have his in a little egg-cup. He'd munch it all down and lick his lips in delight – Errol loved porridge.

The trouble started one day in February. "Don't forget Errol's going to the vet this evening," Jane's mother had said. There wasn't anything wrong with him, but as Jane had never taken him, her mother thought it might be a good idea to go, just to check that they were looking after Errol properly.

They went to the vet's and waited in the waiting room. Errol looked miserable having to sit in a horrible cage and wait his turn to be seen. When they went in the vet was delighted to see such a happy, healthy ratty. "Errol seems very well looked after, to me," he said to Jane. "A little too well in fact. He's a bit on the podgy side; I think he's going to have to go on a diet."

"Oh," Jane said nervously. She wasn't sure Errol would like the sound of that.

"What does he normally have to eat?" the vet went on.

"Well," Jane said, "he starts the day with an eggcup full of porridge . . ."

She didn't get any further. The vet nearly burst with indignation. "Porridge," he spluttered. "You can't give him any more of that. Hamster and gerbil mix and plenty of fruit and veg will be just fine for this young man."

Jane thanked the vet and she and her mother went home with Errol. She hadn't even told the vet about the little marrow dog biscuits Errol liked so much and all the peanuts in the shell she kept in her room for him to eat. It looked as if she was going to have to be very strict with the fat rat.

It was going to be difficult though. Errol had always been an eater. He liked to eat everything and anything. Some of his favorite things weren't even really ratty foods, but he liked them anyway. In the wild, rats will eat anything that's left lying around and in Jane's house, Errol was a bit like that too.

Porridge came top of the list, then peanuts (very fattening), cake and biscuits (a big no-no), dog biscuits (another firm favorite), yoghurt, seeds, berries, and lots of cheese (definitely no more of that allowed!).

The vet had weighed Errol before they left. Errol weighed 500 grams. The vet said Errol should weigh around 300 grams. Errol was much too heavy.

Sometimes it's difficult when you really love an animal like Jane loved Errol. She hated to see him unhappy, but she knew that it wasn't good for him to let him stay so podgy, so she'd have to make him cut down on food one way or another; it nearly broke her heart to see the sad look in his eyes as she tucked into her porridge in the morning and poor Errol had none.

All the family tried to help out with the Errol crisis. Jane's brother Jake made a chart to help her keep a record of just how the diet was going and her mother weighed out specific amounts of food so that Errol would get just enough, and no more. Then Jake devised a training program for Errol. It was an obstacle course, which ran all around the living room. "That'll help him burn off those pounds," he said.

Errol's diet had been going on for two weeks when Jane and her mother first put him in the scale pan to be weighed. "I don't believe it!" Jane's mother sighed, "He's exactly the same as before!"

"How can that be?" Jane cried. "We haven't cheated . . . honestly!"

Another week went by. The strict diet continued. The exercise program went on. Errol should have been turning into a super-lean super-model of the rat world. But instead, when weigh day came, he sat in the pan as fat as he had been the week before! Jane and her family just couldn't work it out until . . . later that day.

Jane's aunt and her husband were coming to stay and that meant Jane's cousin Kate would be coming too and that . . . meant tidying up her room.

When Kate came to stay, they had to do

a bit of furniture re-shuffling, in order to fit an extra bed in. And that's how they discovered just what Errol had been up to! As they pulled the low dressing table out from the wall Errol went bananas! He was running around Jane's feet, squeaking nervously, and quite soon, Jane discovered why.

"Oh Errol," she said crossly, "no wonder you haven't got any slimmer!" There on the floor in front of her was Errol's secret stash of nosh. He had dog biscuits and peanuts galore. A typical rodent, he'd obviously been hoarding his food for sparser times for quite a while before his diet came along, and now he was making use of his handy store-cupboard and keeping himself just as well fed as he had been in his plentiful porridge days.

"Well, that's one mystery cleared up," Jane's mother laughed, "We may be back to square one with the diet, but at least this time we can be pretty sure it's actually going to work!"

And it did: Errol slimmed down to a trim 300 grams and even though there's less of him to love, Jane and Errol still love each other just as much.

Did you know...?

Rabbits don't like their fur being rubbed up the wrong way. Now you know what not to do if you want to avoid having a bad-tempered bunny on your hands!

I love my dog, Candy, so much that when I go
on holiday, I try to phone my neighbour who
looks after her for me, every day, just so that
I can hear her bark and hear her collar rattle.
She's like my best friend, and I miss her loads.

Helen, Ottley

The Tragic Tale of Gelert the Greyhound

WELSH legend tells the tale of a
greyhound that was so loving and
faithful to his lord and master that it
ended up costing him his life.

In the thirteenth century, there was a
Welsh Prince called Prince Llewelyn who
had a beloved greyhound called Gelert.
Gelert was completely devoted to his

master and would do anything to protect him and his family. One day, this devotion was called upon, and the outcome for Gelert was quite tragic.

Llewelyn's wife was busy with her prayers as Llewelyn watched over his baby son. Then the prince heard the huntsman's horn calling him to the chase and decided to go off with the other huntsmen and leave his faithful dog watching over his infant child.

No sooner had Prince Llewelyn left the castle than a hungry wolf came in in search of some tasty morsel to eat. The wolf decided that the baby would make a perfect meal and went into the child's room. Gelert was instantly alert and as the wolf and the hound eyed each other they both knew there was only one way out for them – a fight to the death.

Gelert, usually a sweet-natured dog, fought ferociously. He had to do everything he could to save his master's son from the jaws of death. He suffered terrible injuries at the claws of the great wolf but he fought on, his loyalty and love for Prince Llewelyn overcoming any pain. And, eventually, the battle was over. The wolf lay dead on the floor beside the cradle which had been overturned in the struggle, and Gelert lay panting and injured close by.

When Gelert heard the prince returning, he dragged himself up to greet his master at the door. As the prince came into the room, he was driven almost mad by the scene which lay before him. The wolf was hidden behind a curtain and so all the Prince could see was the upturned cradle and his faithful Greyhound with a muzzle all covered in blood. The Prince momentarily took leave of his senses. Thinking Gelert had killed his only son, he drew out his sword and slew his dog as it stood looking

up at him with trusting, mournful eyes.

Disturbed by all the noise, the baby chose that moment to make his presence under the upturned cradle known, and he gurgled happily to himself. The prince, taken by surprise, rushed over to right the cradle and in so doing saw the body of the wolf lying dead upon the floor.

Suddenly the awful truth dawned on Prince Llewelyn and he realized what a terrible thing he had done. No man had ever been more sorry. But no amount of heartache could ever bring his faithful dog back and Prince Llewelyn realized that Gelert had loved him enough to risk his life for him and yet Llewelyn hadn't even trusted the dog enough to seek the truth before jumping to a terrible conclusion.

Prince Llewelyn had to live the rest of his life carrying the pain and guilt of that one act of madness and as for Gelert, the brave and loving dog is commemorated on a stone in Beddgelert near Snowdon in North Wales. Not only that, but an 18th century ballad retells his story in beautiful rhyme:

'Ah, what was then Llewelyn's pain!
For now the truth was clear;
His gallant hound the wolf had slain.
To save Llewelyn's heir.'

And to this day, thousands of people visit the stone that marks the grave of one of the most loyal dogs of all time.

Perfect Pet Test

Should you get a rabbit or a Rottweiler?

Start here —

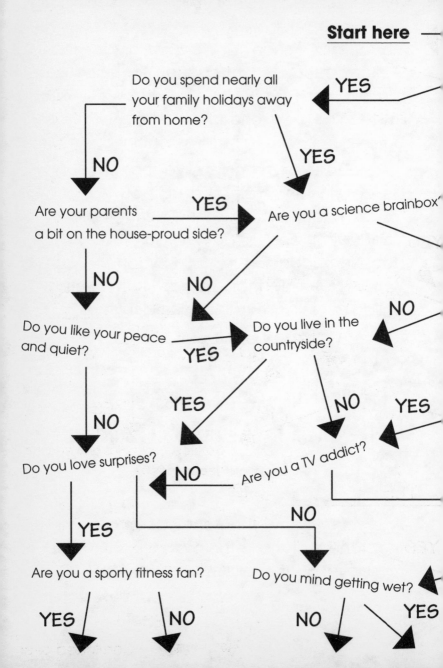

YES

Do you spend nearly all your family holidays away from home?

YES

NO

Are your parents a bit on the house-proud side?

YES

Are you a science brainbox?

NO

NO

Do you like your peace and quiet?

YES

Do you live in the countryside?

NO

YES

NO

YES

NO

NO

Do you love surprises?

NO

Are you a TV addict?

YES

YES

Are you a sporty fitness fan?

NO

Do you mind getting wet?

YES

NO

NO

YES

Find out with this clever critter quiz.

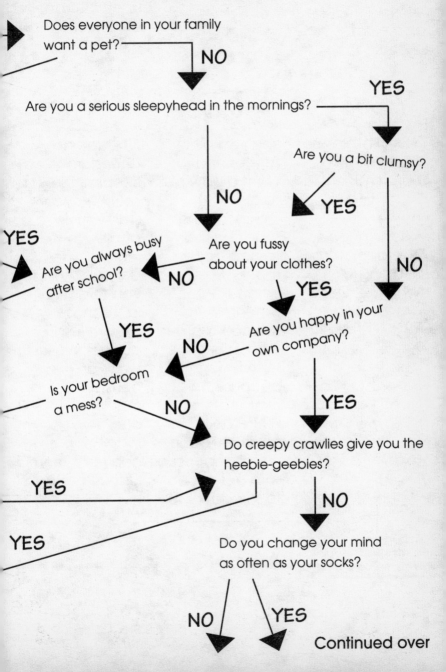

Does everyone in your family want a pet? — **NO**

Are you a serious sleepyhead in the mornings? — **YES**

Are you a bit clumsy?

NO

YES

YES

Are you always busy after school?

Are you fussy about your clothes?

NO

NO

YES

YES

Are you happy in your own company?

Is your bedroom a mess?

NO

NO

YES

Do creepy crawlies give you the heebie-geebies?

YES

NO

YES

Do you change your mind as often as your socks?

NO

YES

Continued over

Are you a sporty fitness fan?

Do you mind getting wet?

YES / NO

NO / YES

Dog

You'd better be full of life if you're planning on setting up home with a lolloping Labrador or a sprinting Whippet. Dogs are loyal and loving but they need top-notch care in return. Love your doggy and your doggy will love you right back, for life!

Cat

You're a bit of a funster and want a paw pal to play with, so look no further than a friendly feline. I hope those of you who said your parents weren't too house-proud were telling the truth though, because one thing cats do like to do is scratch – oooh, watch that new sofa get ripped to shreds!

Fish

Cheap and cheerful, keeping fish is a great way to start your love affair with looking after animals. And, if you're a bit of a lazybones they're just perfect. No long walks or constant mucking out and, if you're really lazy, you can treat them just like the TV!

Do you change your mind
as often as your socks?

NO   YES

Rabbit

A bundle of cuddles who's happy in his own space. If the rest of the family doesn't want a critter round the house, a rabbit's the perfect solution. Happy to live in a hutch in the garden – as long as you keep it out of drafts – Bunny will be your friend for life. Remember though, if you really love your rabbit and want to keep it happy, you've got to give its living quarters a regular clean-out.

Hamster

Too busy for a high-maintenance pet but want something friendly and cuddly which won't need to take over the whole house? Shy Hammy's the one for you. This furball's quite happy left to his own devices; he mainly likes to feed and sleep and gnaw on the interesting things you give him. So go on, be a pet pal and give Hammy a home.

Stick Insect

Easy to keep and feed, stick insects are a very low-maintenance pet for those of you too busy for a creature that might be a bit of an attention seeker. Also, they're fascinating to watch and happy to crawl on you any time you like. Keep them in a tank and try to work out which bit's them and which bit's a . . . well, a stick!

Cat Fact!

Edward Lear, the famous writer and poet, loved his tabby cat, Foss, so much, that he had a second house built that was exactly the same as his first house, so that when he took Foss to stay there, she would feel immediately at home.

Did you know . . .?

 Dogs normally quite like each other. They don't usually want to fight, although sometimes one might chase another one away. On the whole, they just like to have a quick sniff to check out strangers – human or doggy – before deciding they're A-OK!

A Green-Eyed Boxer

Sometimes animals love their human pals so much, they get a bit jealous if any other person or animal seems to become the focus of their owner's affections. Sally

Watkins of Somerset discovered this for herself when her one-year-old Boxer "B" saw her playing with a ten-week-old pup. "B" was absolutely green with envy at the attention the new arrival was being given and decided to take the law into her own hands.

The seventy-pound boxer rushed over to break up the playing pair and sent poor Sally flying with a very impressive head butt. Sally was knocked out for five minutes and ended up in hospital with a touch of concussion and a swollen eye. But Sally didn't blame "B". She realized her poochy pal was simply acting in a fit of serious jealousy and, unfortunately for Sally, the big dog just didn't even know her own strength!

Did you know . . .?

Gerbils can be shy at first, but if you take the time to gently get to know your gerbil, before long it will let you cuddle it to your heart's content. Be prepared to have a few tasty tidbits ready to help kick-start the bonding process!

Mary the Pub Cat

In the Prince of Wales pub in Hackney, there's a cat called Mary. She's a rather lumpy black and white cat who seems perfectly happy in her pub home. She doesn't seem to mind the noise of the jukebox or the smoky air because what she likes best is to find a nice warm lap to curl up on for a snooze, and in a pub . . . there's always plenty of those!

If you love your doggy . . .

You'll always give it plenty of praise when it's good; hugs of love work better than a hundred harsh words.

Pass the Prickly Parcel

A postmistress in Lincolnshire has a whole load of extra-special deliveries on her hands. Elaine Drewrey who runs the village post office has around 80 prickly houseguests, as she's also in charge of nursing the local population of sick and injured hedgehogs! (Hedgehogs are like little porcupines.)

Elaine takes her role as a hedgehog helper very seriously and has even been given permission to turn the back of the post office into an official hospital for the little creatures – she even keeps the intensive-care cases in her own living room!

She's very well placed in her position as guardian of the hedgerows, since postmen on their rounds are often the first to spot hedgehogs that have suffered injuries, lying at the side of the road. With the help of

one of the postmen, Elaine does initial checks on her little wards and gives them immediate vaccinations against parasites, before deciding what further care they may need.

Once they've been nursed back to health, it's time for them to go back to the wild. Elaine always has mixed emotions at that time. She's sad because while she cares for the little hedgehogs, she grows to love them very much; but also she's happy knowing that, through her, they have been given another chance at living a happy and healthy hedgehog life.

And Elaine knows that when the summer comes, she'll find dozens of tiny orphaned hedgehogs arriving on her doorstep, and the love and care will start all over again . . . ahhh!

Cat Fact!

Mark Twain the famous American author thought cats were so fab that he said that if you could cross a man with a cat, it would improve the man but have the opposite effect on the cat!

Did you know . . .?

Dogs like being a bit on the stinky side. If they find something smelly, they like to have a good roll in it. If you love your doggy, you either have to get used to the smell . . . or take some time out to give him a nice cleansing bath!

Kimmi to the Rescue

When their dog, Kimmi, slipped a disk, it was going to cost Mark and Leanne Davies about $1200 for an operation to fix it. They didn't have that kind of money on hand, because there was a new baby on the way, and they knew all the costs that that would mean. But, the alternative was too awful to bear – Kimmi would have to be put down. Rather than see that happen to the eleven-year-old spaniel they loved so much, the couple saved up until they had enough money to pay for Kimmi's treatment.

When the baby was born, they made quite a happy family. Mom, dad, Kimmi the dog, and baby Jenna all got along happily together.

Then, one night in the early hours of the morning. Leanne was woken by Kimmi who was frantically barking and pacing the floor, back and forth to the baby's bed. Leanne got up and went over to where the baby slept, to find Jenna, who was only five weeks old at the time, desperately trying to breathe, her little arms and legs waving and her face turning blue.

Mark and Leanne rushed Jenna to hospital for emergency treatment, where a blockage in her throat was cleared and the baby was able to breathe again. The doctors told them they had been very lucky indeed, since in only another few moments

Jenna might have died. But, thanks to Kimmi, the spaniel with a lot of love in her heart, the whole family are together and happy again. And as for the $1200? Mark and Leanne think that's definitely the best money they've ever spent!

Did you know . . .?

 If your doggy's a real sucker for love, it'll lie on its back as a sign that it trusts you and would just love a stroke on the chest and a gentle tickle on the tummy!

Balto the Brave

IN New York's Central Park, there stands a statue of Balto, the bravest dog there ever was. It was put up in December 1925, almost a year after Balto had performed the heroic deeds that gave him a place forever in the hearts of the American people.

In 1925 Balto, a beautiful, long-haired, black malamute, was the lead dog for a sled team run by a man called Gunnar Kasson. He worked for a gold-mining company and used his sled and team of dogs to ferry supplies back and forth from the frontier town of Nome, far up in the frozen North of Alaska.

It was in this year that disaster struck the little town. A very dangerous disease called diphtheria had been caught by two children in the town. The doctor knew that he needed special medicine to cure the children. Without it they would die. He also knew that diphtheria was a very virulent disease and would spread very quickly and that, if he didn't get the medicine soon, it wouldn't only be the two children whose lives were at risk, but the whole town would be in danger of being wiped out.

The only place he could get the medicine from at that time was the hospital in Anchorage – 800 miles away. They got a message through to the hospital and the medicine was loaded on to a train. But the weather conditions were terrible. Heavy snow had fallen all around and the train struggled to get through. Eventually they had to give up. The train was stuck in the deep snow and the medicine was still 700 miles away from Nome.

The people of the town were in despair. The situation seemed completely hopeless. They were all going to die. Then the suggestion was made that instead of trying to get through with modern transportation, why not rely on the good old traditional methods and bring the medicine in by sled. Teams of dog-sleds could be lined up along the route, like a relay. When one team had done its stretch and was worn out by the snow and cold, they would pass the delivery on to the next team and so on, all the way to Nome.

On January 27, 1925, the race began. Twenty-one dog teams were lined up along the route to Nome. Gunnar, with Balto at the lead, were to take the second-to-last stage at Bluff. From Bluff they would race to Safety where they would meet another team who would take the medicine along the final stretch from Safety to Nome. All of them knew that it was a race against time and they must complete their stages just as quickly as they could.

All the teams along the route waited tensely for their turns to come. So much was at stake that they could hardly sleep for worrying about it. Gunnar knew that his team would be all right with Balto at the lead. He had been chosen as the lead dog because of his strength and intelligence and Gunnar trusted him without question.

As Gunnar and Balto and the rest of the team waited, some of the worst winter storms blew up along the route. The other teams had to battle through terrifying blizzard conditions to get to Bluff, before finally arriving two days late. The town of Nome was running out of time.

When the team they were waiting for finally arrived Gunnar and Balto leapt into action. Gunnar loaded up the medicine as Balto and rest of the team lined up in

front of the sled ready to be harnessed and make their way into the bleak snowy night.

The going was hard. The snow raged around them; they ploughed through neck-high snowdrifts and slipped and skidded on the icy surface of frozen rivers. The snow fell so hard that Gunnar could hardly see his hand in front of his face but, luckily for him, Balto was familiar with the route and led the sled-team safely along their way.

Finally they reached their destination. The

storm had lulled and up ahead of them they saw the waiting point at Safety. Balto had led his team safely there. But, where was the next driver? As they pulled up no one came out to greet them, no other dogs barked on their arrival. Gunnar's heart sank. But there was no time to stand around wondering what had happened to the final team. The people of Nome's lives were hanging in the balance – depending on the sled teams getting the medicine through to them. Gunnar mushed the dogs onward. Balto seemed to know what was needed and with an extra burst of energy charged onward across the snowy landscape, pulling the other dogs behind him.

In the early light of dawn they reached the little town. Balto and his friends had pulled the sled for 20 hours over 53 miles of barren snowy landscape. They were so exhausted they could barely raise a bark to announce their arrival. The vital medicine had been transported right across country in just five and a half days. The town of Nome was saved. The American newspapers carried the story. They were so moved by the strength of Balto and his team – they could hardly believe that one dog could be so brave. It was Balto who had battled through the arctic conditions to get the medicine through and Balto who had restored life to the threatened town.

Everybody loved Balto. And everybody still does!

Did you know . . .?

 If you need to clean your bunny's sensitive bits, like the face, feet, or under the tail, you can make it less stressful for the little fella by sending him to sleep first! Cradle bunny in your arms or across your lap and tip his head backwards, while repeatedly stroking from  the bridge of bunny's nose up to his ears until he's one sleepy wabbit!

Piggy Pal

Susie-Jane Munroe of Nebraska is a friend to all things piggy. She takes in any injured or abused pigs from the surrounding area and gives them the kind of love and support they need. At present she has eight fully-grown pigs and three little squealers.

She can't believe the terrible way some of these animals are treated before they finally make it to her door. One pig (now called Jessie) was thrown from a moving car on the highway and it was only three cars later that anybody actually stopped to see if she was OK.

Two of the littlest pigs help each other out.

Did you know . . .?

That according to the Pet Food Manufacturer's Association, there is scientific evidence that children growing up with a pet develop better social skills and have a greater respect for all living things.

Norma can't see very well and so Alvin does the looking for her. He leads the way and stops her bumping into things and helps her get to the trough on time when they're ready to chow down!

Culture Cats

If you ever have the chance to visit the beautiful city of Rome in Italy, be sure to pop in to the Colosseum where you will see not only a remarkable feat of ancient architecture, but also, a wonderful collection of well-fed stray cats!

It is estimated that in Rome there are around 10,000 cat colonies, many located around the various tourist sites in the city. Although they're strays, these cats are as happy as the best-cared-for pets because since 1988, when a law was passed to protect their rights, they are able to live exactly where they were born, and nobody is allowed to chase them away.

Not only that, but people in the city often provide the cats with leftover pasta for their supper and at least 500 of the colonies are provided with veterinary care either by private animal welfare groups or by the

city's own services.

What a purr-fect life for these happy Italian kitties!

Did you know . . .?

 That cats escape from danger by climbing up trees. Don't worry too much if your cat does this. She'll probably come down in her own good time.

Presidential Pets

If you're ever in Washington, why not check out the White House. This impressive building has been home to some of the most impressive politicians the world has seen but, behind every great leader, there's usually a friendly pet to help out in times of stress!

Bill Clinton has a chocolate Labrador retriever called Buddy, Amy Carter (President Carter's daughter) had a cat called Misty Malarky Ying Yang, and President Lyndon Johnson used to love to have his dog Yuki with him in the Oval Office while he made his world-changing decisions.

But, probably the most famous and best loved of all First Pets, belonged to President Franklin D. Roosevelt. Roosevelt's beloved

Scottish terrier Fala was born on April 7, 1940 and was a gift from his cousin Margaret Stuckley, who had already named him Big Boy. Roosevelt renamed him Murray the Outlaw of Fala Hill – or Fala for short! Fala slept in the President's bedroom and often traveled with him. The President, who had suffered from polio and was often restricted to a wheelchair, rarely went anywhere without Fala. When Roosevelt collapsed and died, Fala jumped up, ran out of the house and up a nearby hill where he stood like stone, refusing to come down. And today, they lie buried next to each other in the rose garden of the grounds of the home they loved.

If you love your doggy . . .

You'll train it properly. A well-trained dog is a safe and happy dog. If your dog's obedient, you'll be able to keep it out of harm's way. And if you love your doggy, that's just what you'll always want to do.

Did you know . . . ?

That Australian scientists have found that the average cholesterol level of patients who were pet owners was two percent lower than those who weren't. Pet owners also had lower blood pressure. That's what love does for you!

Are You Your Pet's Best Friend?

So your mother bought you a bunny. But are you a deserving owner? Or are you a slacker when it comes to pet care? Better put yourself to the test and see if you really are nice enough to give Fido a home . . .

1. Your cat is whinging around your legs for food, four hours before dinner time. Do you

a. Give up instantly and go and get the tin opener? You can't resist those mournful mews.

b. Ignore her and when it is dinner time add on an extra hour? Serves her right for being so annoying.

c. Wait until dinner time and then give her her food? It's best for her to have a routine.

2. Your new puppy has had a fight with a couch cushion and there are feathers everywhere. Do you

a. Go completely nuts, yell at the dog and chuck it outside for the rest of the night?

b. Firmly but gently tell your dog off, making sure it knows it's done wrong and won't make the same mistake again?

c. Give the dog a big cuddle? It's so cute when it's naughty. Then rush around cleaning up the mess before your mother gets home.

3. The man at the shop told you you've only to feed your fish once a day. No more and no less. Do you

a. Feed your fish once a day?

b. Keep forgetting to feed them at all for days on end and then give them a great big pinch to make up for it?

c. Feed them about three times a day –
they're always glubbing around
looking hungry?!

4. It's your turn to clean the rabbit hutch out. Do you

a. Put the rabbit in its run while you
change its bedding, clean up its food
bowl and refresh its water?

b. Spend so much time cuddling your
bunny that you have to give its hutch
a quick once over in about thirty
seconds flat?

c. Just add a bit of new sawdust to the
old stuff – after all, your sister will do it
properly tomorrow?

5. A dog chases your cat up a tree. Do you

a. Stand under the tree crying for the
rest of the day? You're sure Tiddles is
never coming down again!

b. Go inside and forget about it?

c. Watch from the window to give your
cat time to calm down, then try to
coax Kitty down with some tasty
treats?

6. It's your turn to walk the dog. Do you

a. Take Rover around the corner out of sight of your house, tie him to the bench and sit reading your comic for half an hour?

b. Spend the time trying to teach Rover to shake paws with you, only leaving time for a quick dash around the block?

c. Go for a good long walk across the local playing field? It's good for Rover, and it's good for you too!

7. You notice your guinea pig having a vigorous scratch. Do you

a. Instantly assume it's got fleas and rush out and buy every available guinea-pig anti-flea product there is?

b. Take no notice, guinea pigs are always scratching, that's just what they do?

c. Watch your guinea pig carefully for a couple of days to see where and when he usually scratches, and if it doesn't stop, make an appointment with the vet to find out just what the trouble is?

8. When you grow up do you want to be

a. The owner of a doggy beauty parlour? Pampering pooches from dawn to dusk is your idea of heaven.

b. A taxidermist? As far as you're concerned the only good animal is a stuffed animal!

c. A vet? You want to do something caring, yet practical to help your furry and feathered friends.

9. You're off to the seaside for a week of sun and sand. Your best friend is giving a holiday home to your gerbils. Do you

a. Enjoy your holiday, safe in the knowledge that your pal will take good care of your beloved gerbies?

b. Have a fabulous time – no smelly gerbils to have to clean out?!

c. Spend the week pining for your gerbils, only to get home and find they've had a lovely time without you?!

10. Your dog's had puppies. Do you

a. Work hard at finding them all nice loving homes, even if the people can't pay for them?

b. Rub your hands together with glee at the thought of all the lovely money you'll make, and only sell them to the highest bidder?

c. Try and convince your parents that you can keep all six of them, that you'll look after them and buy their food and it'll be just fine...?

Paw Scores

1. A 5   B 0   C 10   2. A 0   B 10   C 5
3. A 10   B 0   C 5   4. A 10   B 5   C 0
5. A 5   B 0   C 10   6. A 0   B 5   C 10
7. A 5   B 0   C 10   8. A 5   B 0   C 10
9. A 10   B 0   C 5   10. A 10   B 0   C 5

0–35

Oh dear, oh dear, oh dear. You really haven't got your pet's best interests at heart at all, have you? You'd be better off having a brick for a pet until you learn to take some responsibility for another little creature's life. Shame on you!

35–70

Ahhhh! There's no doubt about it, you love your pets to death. The only trouble is, you're such a softie that you'll let Rover get away with murder and Tiddles run rings around you, and that's not always best for your pet. Still, there's no doubting your furry friends will be absolutely loved up to the eyeballs!

70–100

What a star pet pal you are. You've really got what it takes to be your pet's best mate. You combine a caring streak a mile wide with a good big dollop of common sense. Your pet's one lucky critter – and that's for sure!

The Hamster Brigade

WHEN Earl and Buffy Templehoff put their three kids Ronnie, Louise, and Mitch to bed one early fall evening they were annoyed to see that Louise had let Norby, the family hamster, out of his cage again. Louise hated to see Norby locked up and was always letting him roam free. Earl and Buffy were convinced it couldn't be hygienic and were always telling Louise not to do it. Louise ignored them. She only wanted Norby to be as happy as he could be.

Earl tutted as he tucked Louise in for the night. Norby could be anywhere and it was too late to start a search now; they'd just have to find him in the morning and then he'd have to go right back in his cage. Louise sighed unhappily. She hated to do it to her little friend, but it looked as if her parents were going to blow a gasket if she didn't start keeping him in his cage permanently. She felt sorry for little Norby as she rolled over and closed her eyes and went fast to sleep.

Louise had no idea what time it was when she first heard Norby's distressed squeaking.

She'd never heard a sound like it. Hamsters were always such quiet sleepy creatures. Whatever could be making Norby behave in such a way? She rubbed her eyes sleepily, trying to get them to see through the dark of the bedroom. Norby was scraping frantically at the door, rushing back and forth across the floor, then squeaking and scraping at the door again, in a state of complete panic. Louise had no idea what was wrong but she shuffled out of bed anyway and in two strides she was across the floor and

beside Norby at the bedroom door. She turned the handle and was stunned by the smell of smoke rising up from the lower floor of the house. The house was on fire!

Norby, meanwhile, had run across the landing to the room that Louise's little brothers shared and was scraping at the door and squeaking wildly. Louise ran across the landing to her parents' room and burst through their door. "The house is on fire!" she yelled, "We've got to get out."

Ronnie and Mitch, woken by Norby's frantic squealing and scrabbling, had emerged sleepily from their bedroom. They stood on the landing looking dazed and confused. Norby ran up to Louise. She picked him up and cradled him safely in her hands as the whole family made their way to the back of the house and the stairs that led down to their backyard.

Foolishly, because they had only recently moved in, the Templehoffs hadn't got around to fitting their smoke detectors yet. Fortunately for them, they seemed to have their own very special smoke detector, in the form of Norby the hamster. Because of his quick actions, their house suffered little damage and they all escaped unharmed. And from that day, not only did they make sure they had properly fitted and working smoke detectors, but they also never argued about keeping Norby in a cage any more. He was a hamster with the run of the house, which seemed like hardly any thanks at all, considering it was to Norby that they owed their very lives.

Did you know . . .?

 That although gerbils originally come from the desert they don't like to be too hot! So keep Gerbie out of the midday sun and he'll be a really happy chappy!

Tug-of-Love

When people get divorced, they often have great difficulty in dividing up the possessions they have collected together over the years. Obviously this is even worse and even more upsetting when there are beloved pets involved. When Paul and Sukie Arenas decided they could no longer go on living together, they were completely devastated at the thought that one or the other of them would have to go on living without their beloved greyhound, Walter.

At first they fought over who had the most right to the smoky grey dog. Sukie had chosen him and picked him up from the local dog's home, but Paul had paid most of the vet's bills. Sukie took him for long walks, but Paul was the one who always put out his food and water. Neither could bear to part with Walter – he was so much a part of both of their lives and even if they didn't love each other any more, they still loved him.

They had no idea what to do; if they were going to live apart, they couldn't both keep Walter, or could they? Eventually, that's just what they decided to do. Walter became a suitcase dog, he spent a month at Paul's and then the following month at Sukie's. At first they were worried that he might not like it and might not settle down, but Walter's a very good-natured and easy-going fellow and he soon seemed to get used to his routine and fitted in quite happily at either household. And what's more he now had two of everything and twice the amount of love!

Did you know . . .?

That some pets get to go for expensive counseling when their owners are getting divorced. A divorce upsets everyone in the family, not just the humans. Dogs, cats and even rats have been known to pick up on the upsetting atmosphere of an unhappy household and have become distressed pets as a result. Nothing that a bit of TLC can't put right though!

I love my cat, Marmalade, because when he was just a kitten he was hit by a car and he lost an eye and damaged his jaw. For about a month he needed my help to feed him. He was so little and fragile and I felt so sad that he'd been hurt, but I felt special being able to look after him and help him get better. We grew so close over that time, and when he was finally able to eat by himself and go out and about again, it was as if he still never forgot the time when he was hurt and unwell and would always come to see me at the end of the day for a cuddle and some love. Some people think he looks funny because he's only got one eye, but to me he just looks special, and I love him all the more.

Jane, Sunderland

Cat Fact!

Ernest Hemingway the famous novelist loved cats so much that he had thirty in his house in Havana. As if that wasn't enough he had another fifty at home in Key West, Florida. Some of his cats had six toes and you can see their descendants still roaming around the old house to this day.

Dogs do their bit

EVERYBODY knows about seeing-eye dogs for the blind and hearing dogs for the deaf, but there's another organization providing specially trained dogs to be the "arms and legs" of people with serious disabilities. Canine Partners for Independence trains dogs (mainly golden retrievers) to perform the tasks their disabled owners can't manage.

The idea started in the USA in the mid-1970s and quickly spread around the world as people realized just what enormous benefit having a doggy partner could be to people with disabilities. Puppies are carefully picked, with their ability to learn quickly only matched by their loving good nature. By the time their training is over they will be able to respond to over ninety verbal commands. They can do everything from opening and closing the curtains and picking up dropped keys to picking the shopping off the shelves at the supermarket and getting cash out at the bank. But much more than that, they provide companionship and love for people who might otherwise feel quite isolated.

There's nothing like taking your dog out for a walk to get people talking to you, and that's the same whether you're a disabled or an able-bodied person. Ian Free, who had a swimming accident when he was just 19, and was left paralyzed from the neck down says that since he got his golden retriever Alex he feels as if his life has begun again. He loves to take Alex out for walks in the park and, through his dog, he has discovered a level of independence he thought he would never again have. Alex even goes to the bar to pay for Ian's drink when they go to the pub together!

Carole and Biggles are another example of how the love of a good dog can turn a person's life around. Carole was a lively young mother of two when out of the blue she suffered a severe stroke, which left her permanently paralyzed on her left side. She felt as if her life had been destroyed; she had very little strength in her body and she could no longer see very well. She went from looking after her home and her family, to being barely able to look after herself. Her husband even had to give up his job to help pull the family through.

Then Biggles came into Carole's life and she's never looked back. He's better around the house than any maid, putting the washing in and out of the machine, helping with the shopping, bringing the phone, and picking up anything left lying around to help her tidy up.

Both Ian and Carole know that they no longer need to worry about how they'll manage certain things in life, as they've got Alex and Biggles to look after them. Their dogs really do mean the world to them, and they love them for it.

If you'd like to know more about Canine Partners for Independence, you can write to them at: Canine Partners for Independence, Homewell House, 22 Homewell, Havant, Hants, PO9 1EE

Did you know . . .?

The same perfume-makers who came up with a scent based on the smell of fresh earth are now working on a fragrance to resemble the warm friendly smell of ickle puppies and kittens. Awwww, isn't that cute!

Desperate Dog Hunt

WHEN Mrs. Marcoolyn of Ipswich in England took her wire-haired fox terrier for his daily walk around the park, she didn't know that it would be the last time she would see Patchie for a whole seven days!

The weather had been gray and wet as they set out on their walk and Patchie, not usually a nervous dog, had nearly jumped out of his skin when a loud clap of thunder had suddenly broken the quiet of the late afternoon. Before Mrs Marcoolyn could do anything to stop him, Patchie hared off into the distance and, as his worried owner rushed after him, he vanished from sight.

The rain began to pour in earnest and Mrs. Marcoolyn and her son walked around the park calling Patchie's name. They searched high and low until they were soaked through to the skin but there was no sign of the poor little dog. They went home to get dry and change their clothes and then they came back to the park and searched again. But it was no good; darkness fell and there was still no sign of Patchie. He had simply disappeared.

The family was so upset. They returned to the park every day to search for their missing dog. They made posters and put them up all around the area in the hope that someone might have seen Patchie and would get in touch. The days went by and the situation seemed more and more hopeless; the whole family was so upset, imagining the worst and thinking that maybe they might never see Patchie ever again.

Then, on the seventh day, Mrs. Marcoolyn got a phone call out of the blue. Patchie had been found! Another dog owner had been out walking when his dog started jumping around excitedly beside an old hollow tree trunk. The person had come to pull the dog away, and had heard the sound of whimpering coming from inside the log. The groundkeepers had come to the scene and, after a bit of digging, had released a rather bedraggled, very hungry, and exceedingly sorry-for-himself Patchie!

Mrs. Marcoolyn and her family were overjoyed! They couldn't believe that every day they'd walked right up close to the old hollow log and Patchie had never made a sound. But none of that mattered now. All that mattered was that they had their little dog back with them where he belonged. And because they don't ever want the same thing to happen again, they're definitely not going to take Patchie out on a thundery day ever again!

Dozy Dormice Need a Nighttime Network

The British Forestry Commission have fallen in love with some sleepy little fellows no bigger than the palm of your hand. The dormouse had had such a tough time of it in its natural habitat that it had nearly become extinct, because of the post-war loss of broad-leafed woodland. But the caring chaps at the Commission have decided to give the dormouse a helping hand. Dormice are nocturnal, but don't like to travel along the ground at night, in case they get nabbed by nasty predators. So they're being built a special dormouse super-highway made from hazel branches that means they can

Did you know . . .?

The happiest bunny of all will be the one with a special big enclosure to run around in. Rabbits are exercise fans and not getting a regular workout will definitely turn bunny into a big ol' grumpy grouch!

go wherever they like, whenever they like. But only for five months of the year mind you – they sleep for the other seven!

Lucky for You

JAN Deever has her Irish setter, Lucky, to thank for the fact that she's alive today. Jan lives on a remote ranch in Montana and for a lot of the time her husband works away from home leaving Jan on her own with lovely Lucky.

But Jan didn't realize just how lucky for her Lucky would be, until the day she took a fall in her kitchen and it was only thanks to Lucky's quick thinking that she made it through at all.

It was a Sunday afternoon; Jan's husband had just set off to the airport for a week working away. Jan decided to do a bit of spring cleaning and tidy her kitchen cupboards, which had needed cleaning out for ages. She pulled up a kitchen stool and climbed on to it. It wobbled precariously, but Jan was always standing on stools to get things out of high cupboards and she hadn't fallen off yet!

She started lifting cans out of the top cupboard; waiting until she had an armload, she bent to place them on the counter below. As she did so, the stool wobbled dangerously. Jan's hands were full and she couldn't grab hold of anything to steady herself. To her horror she felt the stool tipping away from her. She was falling, head first, towards the hard tiled floor.

The last thing she heard as she plummeted downwards was the sound of the cans she had now dropped smashing off the counters, and the sound of her own voice as she let out a terrifying scream and . . . the sound of Lucky, barking in panic, as he watched Jan hit the floor with a heart-stopping thud.

When Jan came around she was woken by Lucky softly licking at her face. Her head was throbbing and at first she had no idea where she was. She felt the cool of the kitchen floor beneath her cheek. Her left arm felt completely numb, but when she tried to move it a pain shot up it that made her cry out. Lucky whimpered beside her. He cocked his head on one side as if trying to work out what Jan wanted him to do, then turned and rushed out of the kitchen. He came back a few minutes later dragging the bedspread from Jan's bed between his teeth. As Jan lay motionless on the kitchen floor, Lucky dragged the bedspread up over his injured owner, carefully adjusting it with his mouth, until Jan was completely covered. Then Lucky ran off again.

Moments later he was back. And Jan was amazed to see that he had the mobile

phone in his mouth. Jan tried to adjust herself so that she could get her right hand into a comfortable position to use the phone. Lucky held the phone in place, his head on one side while Jan dialed 911 for the emergency services. Then Jan took the phone gently from the dog and spoke into the receiver. The paramedics were on their way.

Jan and Lucky lay together on the kitchen floor until they heard the ambulance draw up beside the ranch. Then, it was Lucky who went and opened the door for the ambulance crew, – jumping up to push the big brass doorhandle down. Jan had never realized she had such an amazing dog.

Jan's husband was contacted and came straight back to take care of both Lucky and his wife. And as Jan recovered she often reflected on how lucky she had been to have a dog that wasn't only called Lucky, but was definitely lucky to have around. And another thing Jan thought – I must buy a proper set of steps and stop climbing up on the kitchen stool!

I love my rat Sidney because he's very
intelligent and no matter where I hide his
afternoon snack, he can always find it.

David, Glasgow

Did you know . . .?

That the ancient
Egyptians thought cats
were so cool that they
treated them as gods!

A Truly Troublesome Twosome

WHEN Gabriel McConchie asked
Nancy Trufeau to marry him she
was absolutely delighted. They'd
been seeing each other for quite some time
and both shared the same interests
including . . . their dogs. Gabriel had a Jack
Russell and Nancy had a King Charles
Spaniel, and before they set the date, they
wanted to make sure that their marriage
wouldn't just be a match made in heaven
for them, but for their dogs too.

It was then that things started to go wrong. Whenever they tried to get the dogs together, sparks flew. Bob, the Jack Russell and Barrel the Spaniel, did not get on. Gabriel and Nancy decided to go ahead with their plans anyway, thinking that after a time the dogs would grow to love each other as their owners did, and all would be well. But all was not well, and even after the marriage had taken place, Bob and Barrel were determined not to be friends. Gabriel and Nancy just didn't know what to do. Nancy was still trying to sell her house after moving in with Gabriel and so it was

decided that for the time being she and Barrel should move back there – temporarily – until the dogs made friends. Five years went past and Gabriel and Nancy continued to travel across town between the two houses. But in all that time there was never any question of not keeping either of the dogs. They loved each other, it was true, but they loved their dogs too – too much to ever dream of giving them away over something as silly as having to run two separate homes!

Eventually, Barrel, who was the older of the two dogs, became ill and died. Nancy was devastated; she didn't care that she could now move back in with Gabriel permanently and sell her house. She missed Barrel terribly. And when at Christmas Gabriel gave her a King Charles Spaniel puppy, Nancy cried and cried, remembering her little Barrel who'd been with her through thick and thin. And as for Bob? He didn't seem to mind Louella, the new dog; it seemed he had mellowed in his old age, or perhaps, seeing how happy it made Gabriel to be together with Nancy at last, it finally made him happy too.

I love my hamster, because he's even more sleepy than I am in the mornings!

Gwen, Texas.

A New Home for Flopsy

MRS. KOJEN of London was the head teacher in a nursery. The children were all very small and they loved all animals. They especially loved the nursery bunny Flopsy. Unfortunately for them, Flopsy didn't really love them back! Flopsy was a bit of a nervous rabbit; he didn't like noise and he didn't like bustle – two of the biggest things going on in the world of nursery education.

When the summer holidays came, Flopsy heaved a huge sigh of relief. Six weeks of peace and quiet. He was going home with Mrs. Kojen. Her two children were grown up now and she and her husband didn't seem to go in for the noise and bustle that was so popular at the school.

The six weeks flew by and Flopsy had a lovely time. Mrs Kojen hadn't brought the hutch home as it seemed too much of an effort for such a short stay, and so Flopsy lived life rather like a cat, sleeping in a fluffy bed with a litter tray full of sawdust and straw for his toilet. And he was able to go out and run around in the garden whenever he felt like it.

Then one morning, the six weeks were up. Flopsy sensed it. He could hear Mrs. Kojen getting the travel basket down from the cupboard and he cowered in the corner, his little heart beating hard in his chest. Mr. Kojen saw him and frowned. He was a soft-

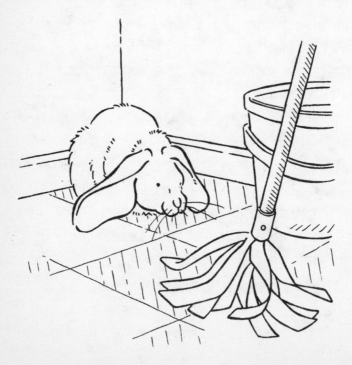

hearted man, and it didn't seem right to him to make the poor rabbit go back to the school if it was genuinely terrified to go.

So when Mrs. Kojen appeared in the kitchen with the travel basket and Flopsy backed even further in to a corner, Mr. Kojen suggested that maybe the rabbit could be given a break and allowed to stay with them. Most of the children would have moved on to proper school by then, he reasoned and it just didn't seem fair to send Flopsy, who had been so happy with them, back to a life of misery at the hands of 40 three-year-olds.

Mrs. Kojen sighed and smiled at her husband. They'd both grown rather fond of Flopsy over the six weeks and rather liked having him around and, it was true, he didn't look too keen to go back to his old life . . . Flopsy was off the hook. He got to stay with the Kojens' for the rest of his days. He would sit and have his ears tickled in the morning as Mr. Kojen read the paper, he would curl up on the couch next to Mrs. Kojen as she watched her favorite soap opera. He was a very, very happy rabbit and they were very happy to have him. And best of all, he no longer had to worry about getting through a day with a lot of noise and bustle – because what he got at the Kojens' was just what he liked best . . . peace and quiet!

Did you know...?

That when your puss is at its happiest and most relaxed, it's likely to be purring with its front paws curled underneath it. Cats usually like to find a nice warm spot to have a snooze in. Is your pussy a pretty purry pal?!

Something Fishy's Going On!

WHEN Sally-ann Myrtle went off to summer camp she knew she was just going to have the best time! Her friends Megan and Sue would both be there and Megan had been to this camp the year before and she said it was just the best. The only thing that was going to take a little shine off her break was the fact that she'd just got two new goldfish. She'd begged and begged for years to be allowed to have a pet but the answer was always the same – a great big no! But eventually her parents had broken down under the strain and agreed she could have something easy to take care of. That's where Merlin and Fred came in. Merlin was a pretty straightforward goldfish but Fred was a red-cap – sort of pinky white with a cap of deep red on his head.

Sally-ann loved her fish. She carefully fed them their pinch of food in the morning. She happily changed their water and cleaned the filter on the tank. She loved to watch them gliding gracefully through the water. She knew they weren't everyone's idea of a dream pet but to her they were just the best – even if TV could be boring as anything, watching Merlin and Fred certainly never was! She had watched them so much, she was familiar with everything about them. The ragged edge to Merlin's front fins, the little extra dot of red next to Fred's red cap, and the way they scooted up to the surface as soon as she lifted the lid of the tank – sure that food was on its way.

Camp was fun and the weeks went quickly by. Sally-ann phoned home often, and always remembered to check how Merlin and Fred were getting on. Her mother always said they were doing just fine. So, it came as a terrible shock to Sally-ann to get home and find that Merlin and Fred weren't doing just fine. In fact, Merlin and Fred weren't even there at all, and swimming in their place were two Merlin and Fred look-alikes. Impostors in the tank! Sally-ann was so upset she cried and cried. Her parents didn't know what to do. Merlin and Fred had got some kind of fungal infection while Sally-ann had been away. Her parents had done everything they could to save them: they'd even driven through to the big aquaria shop in the next town to get medicine. The fish seemed to perk up for a little while but, when her parents got up to look at them the next day, the fish had both died.

Poor Sally-ann's parents just didn't know what to do. They knew how much the fish meant to Sally-ann and they couldn't bear the thought of her coming home to find that they were no longer there. So, they decided to replace them. To them, the fish they had bought looked exactly the same as the original Merlin and Fred, but little did they know how much their little girl loved her fish and just how well she knew them.

When Sally-ann calmed down a bit she had to forgive her parents. She knew they had only done what they'd done to save upsetting her, but she would rather have known the truth. The real Merlin and Fred had been buried at the bottom of the garden, so Sally-ann was able to make them a little headstone and visit them whenever she felt like it. Sally-ann grew to love the new Merlin and Fred and loved to sit by the tank and watch them swimming in their watery world, but despite having these two new friends, she never forgot her first fishy loves – the original Merlin and Fred.

Did you know...?

If your cat gets into a fight with another cat, you should gently check it for any cuts that might be hidden by its fur. Why can't kitties be nice to each other?!

Mikey the Wonder Dog

WHEN Josh Rialto set out with his dog Mikey for a walk in the early fall dusk, he felt pretty happy. The weather was fine, he had been picked for the soccer team, and Carole Andrews who sat next to him in Geography had agreed to go to the movies with him at the weekend. Everything in life was looking up for him. Little did he know it was soon going to start looking down . . . big time!

Josh had got Mikey when he was just a puppy. The big German shepherd had once been a funny ball of fur, lolloping around on legs that seemed too big for his body, with great big paws that he hadn't quite grown into yet. Josh and Mikey did everything together. Josh was pretty sporty – he went running and played soccer, and Mikey was a familiar figure running up and down the sideline, barking his support. Josh's parents never worried about him wandering far afield, as they knew he always had Mikey by his side, watching over him and keeping him safe.

Josh lived on the edge of the town; the front of his house overlooked the main road that circled the outskirts of the town and then, across from that, lay a large open field behind which were great, leafy woods. Josh and Mikey were heading across to the woods. The leaves were turning to the deep reds and oranges of that time of year, and Josh breathed the smell of the damp earth deep into his lungs. Mikey ran ahead, his large tail swishing behind him, his tongue lolling in his mouth as he bounded through the woods. Josh was in his running clothes and jogged to keep up with Mikey. It had been raining heavily for days though, and the ground beneath his feet was slippery and thick with mud. Josh was glad he'd put his old sneakers on: he'd ruin his new ones running through this stuff.

Josh and Mikey had run through the woods together so many times that they knew every winding trail and path, and tonight Josh was going to do the long circular route. He was heading towards the large valley in the center of the woods where the path thinned to a narrow ledge, carved out of the side of the deep ravine. As Josh ran to the sharp corner that led to the narrow path, Mikey stopped dead in his tracks just ahead of him, barking and whining. Josh tried to stop, thinking he'd run into the large dog if he didn't, but he was going too fast and, as he swung around the corner, he realized what had made Mikey stop so suddenly – the heavy rain had caused a landslide of the muddy earth. The path was gone.

Josh tried to skid to a halt, the ground giving way under his shoes, his arms flailing wildly as he tried to regain his balance. He could feel himself falling backwards into the deep ravine below. He yelled out in terror as something yanked him backwards and the thin material of his running top caught sharply against his throat. Mikey had caught him. Mikey was holding fast onto the back of Josh's top and trying to drag him backwards to safety. But, as he did so, Josh heard a terrible tearing noise as the material of his T-shirt ripped apart and he slid terrifyingly quickly towards the bottom of the valley.

It seemed like hours that Josh lay there. He'd tried to get up, but there didn't seem to be a single part of him that wasn't in pain. Still, he thought, it could have been much worse, at least he'd only slid down, – if Mikey hadn't caught him the way he did he would have really fallen. He'd probably be dead. He groaned at the thought, his head throbbing.

It was dark now and cold and Josh lay miserably wondering how long he'd been there and whether help was on its way. He'd heard Mikey barking right after he'd fallen, but after that there was silence. Surely he could trust Mikey to get help.

When he saw the flashlights shining, Josh thought he might cry. He summoned all the strength he had left and called out to his would-be rescuers. But before he could finish shouting, a familiar sound greeted his ears and Mikey stood barking high above on the top of the bank. Mikey had saved Josh not once but twice that day, and that was something Josh would never forget as long as he lived.

Cat Fact!

Sir Winston Churchill, the Prime Minister of Britain during the Second World War, had a beautiful marmalade tom cat that he loved to bits. The cat was Winston's absolute favorite companion and kept his feet warm in the dark wartime nights by sleeping at the foot of Churchill's bed!

Did you know....?

Dogs have loud barks and excellent hearing and they're also ever so loyal to the family they love. What a great burglar alarm!

Why not start your own collection of amazing pet facts?

Did you know....?

Did you know....?

Did you know....?

Did you know....?

Did you know....?

Did you know....?

Did you know....?

Did you know....?

Did you know....?

Did you know....?

Did you know....?

Did you know....?

Did you know....?

Did you know....?

Did you know....?

Did you know....?

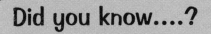

Did you know....?